641.3   Booth, David.
BOO   Eats

PERMA-BOUND   BAR: 478367

DATE DUE			

Eats

DAVID BOOTH

Editorial Board
David Booth • Joan Green • Jack Booth

STECK-VAUGHN
Harcourt Achieve

www.HarcourtAchieve.com

10801 N. Mopac Expressway
Building # 3
Austin, TX 78759
1.800.531.5015

Steck-Vaughn is a trademark of Harcourt Achieve Inc. registered in the
United States of America and/or other jurisdictions. All inquiries should
be mailed to Harcourt Achieve Inc., P.O. Box 27010, Austin, TX 78755.

Rubicon © 2006 Rubicon Publishing Inc.
www.rubiconpublishing.com

Project Editors: Miriam Bardswich, Kim Koh
Editorial Assistant: Kermin Bhot
Art/Creative Director: Jennifer Drew-Tremblay
Assistant Art Director: Jen Harvey
Designer: Jeanette Debusschere

6 7 8 9 10   5 4 3 2 1

Eats
ISBN 1-41902-386-1

CONTENTS

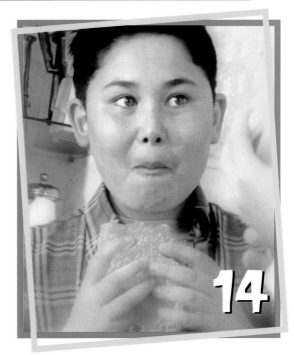

14

25

43

GOOD EATS AHEAD!

This book is about food,
food we enjoy,
food we don't like,
food that we wish we could eat all the time.

Some words will be sweet,
and some will be sour,
some will be good for you,
and some hard to swallow.

So put on your reading bib,
and dig right in!

Yuk Yum Interlocbphoto Box Getty Images/Photo Disc/ANN0868; Girl: Getty Images/Photo Disc/dv24/09

CHEWABLE CHANTS

warm up

What singing ads about food and treats do you know from radio or television? Try singing one to your group.

AIR CONDITIONING

Crush the ice,
Pile it up.
A snow-cone treat
In a freeze-filled cup.

Flavor-filled
slurps and sips,
An Arctic blast...
        Then

        frozen lips!

BELLY UP TO THE BAR

Chugalug
Chugalug
Cool root beer in a mug.

Burping once,
Burping twice,
Nothing left but bits of ice.

A VEGETABLE CHANT

Cauliflower, Cauliflower
Sis boom bah!
Broccoli, Broccoli
Rah rah rah!
Toss them in the garbage ...
Hah hah hah.

Jell-O FANATIC

Wiggle and squiggle
O what a sight!
A bowlful of pleasure
Jiggle delight.

Jell-O for breakfast,
Jell-O at noon,
Jell-O for dinner,
Spoon after spoon.

Dreaming of Jell-o
I lie in my room.
There through my window —
A round Jell-O moon.

wrap up

1. Work in small groups. Each group chooses a chant to practice. Add some movement, like cheerleaders do, and present your chant to the class.

2. Conduct a short survey of your classmates to find out their favorite vegetable, drink, and Jell-O flavor. Record results on a three-column chart. Tally the results and name the Top Favorite in each category.

Take a TASTe!

warm up

What is the sweetest food you have ever tried? What is the most sour food you have ever tasted? What is the spiciest food you have ever tried? What is the saltiest food you have ever eaten?

Look closely at your tongue. You'll see that the top of your tongue is covered with lots of little bumps. These bumps are called papillae (puh-pil-ee). They help grip food and move it around while you chew. Inside the papillae are your taste buds. People are born with about 10,000 taste buds.

Each taste bud is made up of tiny hairs that can tell whether food is sweet, sour, salty, or bitter. Different parts of your tongue are more sensitive to certain tastes. Most people taste sweet on the tips of their tongues, sour on the sides, bitter on the back, and salty near the front and sides. However, any part of your tongue can sense any kind of taste. Try the experiment on the next page.

CHECKPOINT

Where on your tongue do you think you would taste something that's both sweet and sour?

sensitive: *easily affected*

FYI

Things like cold foods or drinks can make your taste buds less sensitive. If you ate an ice pop made of juice, it would not taste as sweet as plain juice.

The cells that make up taste buds are replaced every 10 days.

All Images–Istockphoto

Experiment: Parts of the tongue are sensitive to certain tastes

What you'll need:

Cotton swabs

(A) Salt water   (B) Sugar water

(C) Lemon juice   (D) Onion juice

1. Draw a chart to record your results. Along the left side, write the names of all four solutions you will taste. Across the top, draw three columns and label with front, back, and sides.

2. Dip a cotton swab into liquid (A) and lightly touch the front part of your tongue. Taste the liquid.

3. Drink a little water to clear your tongue of the taste.

4. Take a new cotton swab and dip it in liquid (A). Now dab it on the back part of your tongue. Taste the liquid and sip some water. Then try it again on the sides of your tongue.

5. Which part of your tongue tasted the liquid the strongest? Write down your results on the chart.

6. Repeat the same process for liquids (B), (C), and (D).

7. Draw a map of the tongue and indicate the parts that were the most sensitive to the four tastes. Compare your map with a friend's. Did you both taste the same things on the same parts of your tongues?

wrap up

Conduct the experiment with your classmates. Create a "tasting center" in your classroom and record your own results. Were there any differences in the results?

WEB CONNECTIONS

Why do babies spit out strong tasting food? Use the Internet to search for the answer.

THE STORY OF POTATOE

warm up

- Where do you think people found and ate the first potato? In Ireland? In North America? In China?

- What food do you and your family eat that is imported from another country? Why don't we grow all our own food where we live?

The Origin

We know the potato was first grown in South America because scientists have found potato remains in the ancient ruins of Peru and Chile. The potato was important in Incan culture. Not only was it worshipped but it was buried with their dead. The Inca word for potato is "papas."

1540

Spanish conquistadors first saw the potato when they arrived in South America. Spanish soldier and historian Pedro de Cieze de Leon wrote about them in his book *Chronicles of Peru*.

conquistadors: *explorers*

1565

Spanish explorer and conqueror Gonzalo Jimenez de Quesada came to South America looking for gold. Instead he found potatoes. Realizing their value, he took them to Spain. Potatoes were soon eaten aboard Spanish ships.

1580s

The potato slowly spread to other European countries. It reached England and Italy around 1585 and two years later it was in Germany and Belgium. However, most people treated the potato with suspicion and fear.

ITALY

ENGLAND

BELGIUM

GERMANY

FRANCE

1588

An Irish legend says that ships of the Spanish Armada, wrecked off the Irish coast, were carrying potatoes and that some of them washed ashore.

1589

The potato was probably first brought to Ireland by Sir Walter Raleigh. He planted them at his Irish estate. By the end of the 1600s, all the peasants in Ireland were growing and eating potatoes.

1719

Potatoes were planted in the United States by Scottish and Irish immigrants. Potatoes soon spread all over the country.

FYI

When Thomas Jefferson became President of the United States, he started serving a dish he had eaten in France. The dish was called *pommes frites* — otherwise known as French fries. Before becoming president, Jefferson had been minister to France where he had tasted the fries.

1770s

The wife of French King Louis XVI often pinned potato flowers in her hair. Other ladies in the court took up the fashion and wore potato blossoms in their hair.

1836

Idaho is known the world over for its potatoes. The first potatoes were planted in Idaho by Henry Harmon Spalding, a missionary.

1845–1849

The Irish Potato Famine, also called The Great Famine, struck in Ireland. It was caused by heavy rain, which rotted the potatoes in the ground. This destroyed a major source of food for most of the population. It caused over one million deaths.

1850s

Americans still think the potato is not fit for humans and should be fed to animals.

1872

The most common potato in the U.S. today is the Russet Burbank. It was developed in 1872 by horticulturist Luther Burbank. The potato soon started appearing all over Idaho and helped the Idaho potato industry really take off.

horticulturist: *a person skilled at growing plants*

wrap up

1. Create a timeline using a long piece of cord, file cards and clothes pins in your classroom. Write on each card the information connected to one date. Add a card for 1995 and 2005. What information will you put on the card?

2. What three surprises did you find in the information? Why do you think these facts seem so unusual?

13

THE SAUCE BOSS

FYI

According to the *Guinness Book of World Records*, the world's hottest spice is the Red Savina Habanero. It has a rating of 350,000–570,000 on the Scoville scale (an index for measuring the hotness of chilies). In comparison, the jalapeno has a score of only 2,500–5,000.

warm up

- In your family who likes their food: mild, spicy, very hot?

- What are some problems with eating outside at a picnic or a barbecue? Ants? Weather? _____? _____? _____?

14

It's barbecue time,
It's barbecue fun,
Hamburgers and hot dogs
For everyone!

To top it all off,
A tangy touch,
A special sauce,
Always too much!

RUN!
The boss has found the sauce!
The boss has found the sauce!

That sauce is hot
It attacks your tongue,
Your lips swell up,
Your teeth are numb!

New rule!
No more sauce
For me or you,
Just plain meat
On the barbecue.

wrap up

1. With your group, prepare for a readers'
   theater presentation. Decide who you will
   be as you say the words. How will you
   show who the Sauce Boss is?

2. What words rhyme with these words?
   boss! _____   rule! _____
   fun! _____   spice! _____
   up! _____   thumb! _____

FOOD FACTS

warm up

Most of us take food for granted. But much of the food we eat was created or found by accident. What strange sandwich have you designed? What is the strangest-looking food you have ever seen?

The **cheeseburger** was first made in 1934 at Kaelin's Restaurant in Louisville, Kentucky. The restaurant, Kaelin's, is still in business. They cook their burgers in an iron skillet, not on a grill.

Until the 1500s, not many people had heard of **tomatoes**. This is because they only grew in the Americas. Until then, the Italians had been putting carrot sauce on their spaghetti.

Haggis is the national dish of Scotland. It is made by mixing sheep's heart, liver, and lungs, with onions, suet, and oatmeal. This mixture is stuffed inside a sheep's stomach and boiled!

The average ear of **corn** has 800 kernels arranged in 16 rows.

BBQ: In the West Indies, people used the word *barbacoa* to describe a wooden grill. The grill was a frame made of wooden sticks placed over a fire in order to cook meat. However some people believe that the word barbecue actually comes from the French word *barbe à queue,* which means "beard-to-tail," i.e. cooking the whole animal over a fire.

16

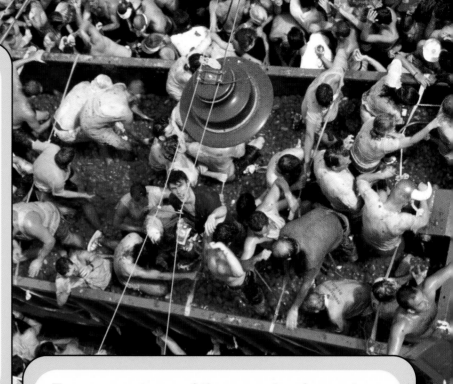

The **potato chip** was invented in 1853 by a chef, George Crum. One day, a diner complained that the French fries were too thick. Crum made a thinner batch, but the customer was still not happy. Hoping to annoy the fussy customer, Crum made fries that were too thin to eat with a fork. The customer, surprisingly enough, was happy — and potato chips were invented!

Every year tens of thousands of people gather in the small town of Bunol, Spain, for … a **food fight**! On the last Wednesday of August, this little village stages a tomato war. For two hours, people pelt one another with ripe, juicy tomatoes. It is the world's largest annual food fight and is part of the La Tomatina festival.

The most expensive **coffee** in the world is *Kopi Luwak*. It is made with the help of small catlike creatures called palm civets. The animals eat the raw red coffee cherries "cleaning" them as they pass through their body. The soft outer part of the coffee cherry is digested. The inner beans are passed out. Locals scoop up the precious poop and sell it! These beans are grown in the Indonesian islands.

Ketchup was first created in China. It was called *ke-tsiap* and was a pickled fish sauce. It then traveled to Malaysia and Indonesia. In the 17th century, English sailors discovered it and took it West. Tomatoes were added to the recipe in the 1700s.

wrap up

Go to the library or use the Internet to research a food you like to eat. Write a food fact about the item.

WHEN FOOD GETS FUNNY!

Customer: Waiter, have you got frogs' legs?

Waiter: Certainly, sir.

Customer: Then hop into the kitchen and get me a steak!

Q What is the father of all corn?

A Popcorn.

Q What did the sign in a restaurant window say?

A EAT NOW — PAY WAITER.

Q Why did the tomato turn red?

A He saw the salad dressing.

Customer: What is this insect in my soup?

Waiter: I wish you wouldn't ask me, sir. I don't know one bug from another.

Q What kind of apple isn't an apple?

A A pineapple.

Illustration By Angela Hodge

HOW TO MAKE ICE CREAM IN A BAG!

warm up

- Brainstorm and list food or drink that comes in a bag.

- Work in small groups. List as many actual flavors of ice cream (they have to be sold in stores) as you can. Which group named the most flavors?

FYI

Ernest Hamwi is often credited for the invention of the ice cream cone. In 1904, Hamwi was at the St. Louis World's Fair selling a crisp, waffle-like pastry. Next to him was an ice cream vendor. Soon the vendor ran out of dishes to serve his ice cream. Hamwi solved his problem by rolling his waffles in the shape of a cone to hold the ice cream, and the cone was born!

WHAT YOU'LL NEED:

1 tablespoon sugar

1/2 cup milk or half & half

1/4 teaspoon vanilla

6 tablespoons rock salt

Small ziploc plastic bag

Large ziploc plastic bag

Ice cubes

STEPS:

1. In the small bag, mix the milk, sugar, and vanilla. You can also add any frozen fruit you like. Then seal it.

2. Fill the large bag half full of ice, and add the rock salt. Seal the bag.

3. Place the small bag inside the large one and seal again carefully.

4. Shake until mixture turns into ice cream, about 5 minutes.

WIPE OFF TOP OF SMALL BAG, THEN OPEN CAREFULLY AND ENJOY!

Want to know how ice cream is traditionally made?

WHAT YOU'LL NEED:

2 eggs
1 cup milk
1 cup sugar
1/8 teaspoon salt
1 cup heavy cream
2 teaspoons vanilla

STEPS:

1. In a small saucepan, mix the egg, milk, sugar, and salt until they are well-blended.

2. Stir the mixture constantly over very low heat till it thickens.

3. Put it in the refrigerator and make sure it is completely cool.

4. Using a mixer, mix the heavy cream and vanilla in a large bowl until stiff peaks form.

5. Remove the egg mixture from the refrigerator and gently add it to the whipped cream until it is well blended.

6. Empty the mixture into a container. Cover the container and place it in the freezer for about 4 hours or until the ice cream is firm.

wrap up

1. Find out how the ice cream is created in the first recipe. What does rock salt have to do with turning ice into ice cream?

2. Try out these recipes at home, or in your classroom. Report if you succeeded in making the ice cream, or if things did not work out.

WEB CONNECTIONS

Visit **http://magma.nationalgeographic.com /ngexplorer/0304/articles/mainarticle.html** to read about the history of ice cream and how it was invented. Choose the five most important dates in the timeline and present them to the class.

I Want a Drink of Water!

warm up

- What is "bottled water"?

- What needs to be done to water before it comes from your tap?

Water is an important part of our daily lives. About 72 percent of our body is made up of water. To stay healthy, it is important to drink around eight glasses of water a day. A person can live more than a month without food, but cannot survive more than a week without water.

For drinking purposes, we need water that does not contain too much salt, or chemicals, or harmful bacteria. Some people choose to drink bottled water rather than water from the tap or cooler.

Bottled Water

Bottled water companies buy their water from an approved water source, such as a city water supply. Some companies get their water from a well or a spring. All companies treat their water to remove harmful substances.

FYI

In the U.S. the National Sanitation Foundation International is an organization that develops standards and certifies that a product is safe for the public.

Background, Bottle of Water—istockphoto; Girl—Getty Images/ Brand X pictures/BXP45654

Is my bottled water safe?

Make sure your bottle has the National Sanitation Foundation International (NSF) mark on the label and is certified. Check that your bottled water still has the factory seal before drinking it. Do not drink from any bottle where the seal has been broken.

How long can I store bottled water?

Bottled water can be stored for a long time. It should be kept in a dry place, out of direct sunlight. It is also necessary to keep it away from toxic chemicals. Do not store bottled water in your garage.

toxic: *harmful*

23

Did you know?

Some of the differences between bottled water and tap water are: the source of the water, its taste, and the way it is treated or purified.

Many people think that tap water has a bad taste because of the chlorine that cities use to treat it.

If a company chooses to add anything to the water, such as minerals, fluoride, or flavorings, they must say so on the label.

Health agencies check bottled water to make sure it is safe. They look for the taste, odor, and color of the water. They also check for chemicals and bacteria in the water.

Around 25-60 gallons of water are used during a five-minute shower.

Water from a tap sometimes looks cloudy, but quickly clears up. This is because there are tiny air bubbles in the water, similar to the bubbles in carbonated soft drinks. After a while, the bubbles rise to the top and are gone leaving the water clear.

wrap up

1. What water do you drink
   a) at a cottage?
   b) on a car trip?
   c) on a bike ride?

2. Have you ever experienced a time when water was scarce? What did you and your family have to do?

WEB CONNECTIONS

Visit **www.epa.gov/safewater/kids/games.html** and click on "Water Filtration: Follow a Water Drop" to find out about the water treatment cycle. Write a short report on what you learned.

NO MORE PORRIDGE!

warm up

- Do you like porridge for breakfast? What does the word "porridge" make you think of?

- Have you ever watched a magician perform magic? What tricks did he/she do? Is there such a thing as "magic"?

This magician guy
knew how to make porridge in a huge pot,
and his pot was never empty.
That is why he was called a magician.

To start the pot cooking, he said
    some magic words.
And the porridge kept coming.
The pot was never empty.

To stop the pot, he said some more magic words.

Well, one day, the magician's helper turned into a spy.
He watched the magician through the keyhole,
and saw him start up the porridge pot.
He heard the magic words!

Quickly, the helper stepped out the back door.
    Now he knew the magic words.
    He could make all the porridge he wanted!

    That night, he crept into the kitchen.
    First he started the fire.
Then he put the pot over it.
Then he said the magic words.

    It worked! ⬅

CHECKPOINT
What do you think is going to happen next?

Illustrations By Mike Rooth

25

The porridge in the pot began to bubble.
And bubble!
And bubble!
Until it flowed out of the pot!

The magician's helper didn't know the words
to shut off the cooking pot!
What a mistake!

The porridge in the pot continued to bubble.
The thick, gooey porridge
Slid onto the floor and out the door!
The porridge rumbled down the path
Into the village and buried it whole.

Anyway, the magician's helper's ghost
is hiding in my house.
Somewhere.

I know he is.

'Cause every morning
He starts the porridge pot
on our stove.

And there's always too much!

Of course, my sister and I have to eat all the porridge.

And why do we have to?

We want honey-covered cereal!

CHECKPOINT
Why does the writer think there is a
ghost hiding in his or her house?

wrap up

1. Retell this story as a storyboard. Use no more than six frames.

2. Is it fair to tell the secret of a magician's trick because you happened to find out how he did it? Yes, because _____. No, because _____.

Moon Cake Message

Illustrated by DREW NG

- Have you ever had a Chinese fortune cookie? Do you remember the message?

- Why would a "spy" hide a message inside some food?

LONG, LONG AGO THE MONGOLS INVADED AND CONQUERED CHINA. THEY TREATED THE CHINESE VERY HARSHLY. OVER TIME, THE CHINESE PEOPLE BECAME ANGRY AND WANTED TO DRIVE THE MONGOLS OUT OF CHINA.

TWO MEN DISCUSS WHAT MONGOLIAN RULE HAS DONE TO THEIR LIVES ...

HOW LONG ARE WE GOING TO TAKE THIS INJUSTICE? WE ARE BEING TREATED LIKE SLAVES!

WHAT CAN WE DO? THE MONGOL KING HAS COMPLETE CONTROL OVER THE CITY.

THERE HAS TO BE SOME WAY WE CAN FIGHT BACK. WE MUST PLAN AN ATTACK.

BUT HOW?

FYI

The Moon Festival is a mid-autumn festival celebrated on the 15th day of the 8th month of the Chinese calendar. On this day the full moon is closest to the Earth, and looks larger and brighter than at any other time of the year. Traditionally, family members gather to admire the moon and eat moon cakes.

wrap up

THE REVOLT WORKED AND THE CHINESE PEOPLE WON BACK THEIR COUNTRY.

1. Why did the revolt work in China? Explain in the form of an announcement by the leader.

2. What viewpoint has the artist used to draw each frame? Draw one frame of the story from a different angle, e.g. from the top, as a bird would see it.

Friends and Food

My friends come from different parts of the world. I get to try their food when I am invited over for dinner.

warm up

- What do your friends eat at their homes that you don't have at yours?

- What food have you eaten that took courage to try?

I get to eat a lot of Greek food at my friend Helen's house. I've eaten souvlaki, dolmas, hummus, and pita bread.

Souvlaki is pieces of flavored meat grilled on a skewer. Pita is a flat, round bread.

Dolmas are grape leaves wrapped around spiced rice. Hummus is a thick dip made from chickpea paste flavored with lemon and garlic.

GREEK GREEK GREEK GREEK

Boy Smiling–Getty Images/ Digital Vision/dv3330001a; All Other Images–Istockphoto

31

At my friend Juan's house, I get to eat all kinds of Mexican food. I've eaten spicy tacos and chimichangas.

FYI

Guacamole is a sauce or dip made from avocados that can be added to almost any Mexican dish.

My favorite dish is chimichangas. They are deep-fried burritos filled with rice, refried beans, cheese, and meat.

Tacos are tortillas (kind of flat bread) filled with meat, salsa, guacamole, and other toppings. You can use just about anything as a filling for your taco.

On the opposite side of the street live Rani and her family. I love going over to their house for dinner. Rani's family is from southern India where they traditionally eat with their hands, and food is served on a banana leaf! I've tasted all kinds of curries made with vegetables or meat that are usually eaten with rice. Along with the curry, we have pappadums. Pappadums are thin, crisp, spiced chips.

My friend Reiko's family is from Japan. When he invites me to dinner, it is like eating at a wonderful restaurant. We use chopsticks to eat and the food is beautifully arranged on the plates. Some Japanese dishes I've tasted are miso soup, sushi, sashimi, and noodles.

Miso soup with white rice is traditional Japanese food. They drink it right from the bowl. Miso is a thick paste made of soybeans, grains, and salt.

Sushi is raw or cooked fish, shellfish, or vegetables wrapped in rice. Sashimi is seafood thinly sliced, served with a dipping sauce. Most sashimi dishes are served raw.

wrap up

1. In which of these four houses would a vegetarian have the most to eat?

2. Draw a map of where your friends and relatives live. On each house you drew, write the special foods they serve when you visit.

On Top of Spaghetti

By Tom Glazer

warm up

What do you think of when you hear the word "spaghetti"?

On top of spaghetti all covered with cheese,
I lost my poor meatball when somebody sneezed.

It rolled off the table, it rolled on the floor,
And then my poor meatball rolled out of the door.

It rolled in the garden and under a bush,
And then my poor meatball was nothing but mush.

The mush was as tasty as tasty could be,
And early next summer it grew to a tree.

The tree was all covered with beautiful moss.
It grew great big meatballs and tomato sauce.

So if you eat spaghetti all covered with cheese,
Hold on to your meatball and don't ever sneeze.

wrap up

1. Sing the song all together. Pretend to sneeze at the end of the song.

2. Write another song using this pattern. Leave out the words spaghetti and meatballs. E.g.: On top of fried rice all covered with spice, I lost my poor shrimp, it wasn't so nice ...

WEB CONNECTIONS

For fun facts about all kinds of pasta, visit **www.ilovepasta.org/factsaboutpasta.html**.

How would you rate your table manners? Take this quiz to find out.

1 When there is only one cookie left on the plate, you:
a) grab it quickly before someone else can.
b) offer it to everyone else at the table before taking it.
c) shout "It's mine!"

2 If you don't like something on your plate, you:
a) gag and spit the food out.
b) feed it to your dog.
c) leave it on one side of your plate.

3 When you are not eating, what do you do with your hands?
a) Put them on your lap or on the table.
b) Play with the forks and spoons.
c) Put them in your pockets.

4 At dinner, when should you start eating?
a) As soon as food is on the table.
b) When everyone has been served.
c) As soon as you sit down.

5 When a piece of food falls off your plate, you:
a) put it on the corner of your plate.
b) don't touch it and leave it on the table.
c) pick it up and eat it.

6 When you want to show your appreciation for a meal, you:
a) chew loudly and burp.
b) stuff yourself with more servings.
c) compliment the chef/host.

7 If you need to pick food out of your teeth, you:
a) excuse yourself from the table and go to the bathroom.
b) use your fork to get the food out.
c) play show and tell with your food.

8 Someone makes your favorite meal, you:
a) take the bowl and empty it on your plate.
b) wait for everyone else to serve themselves.
c) eat as much as possible until you get sick.

9 When your hands are dirty after dinner, you:
a) wipe them on your clothes.
b) lick the food off your fingers.
c) excuse yourself from the table and go to the bathroom.

wrap up

1. Try answering each of the nine questions. Could there be more than one right answer?

2. Create a list of manners for your school lunchroom. Don't be too fussy. Be sure the manners can be followed by everyone. Choose ideas that make the lunchroom a better place.

Turn to page 48 for the answers.

Sonya Thomas chews her way towards a 2004 championship during Philadelphia's annual Wing Bowl chicken wing eating contest. She ate 167 wings, beating Ed "Cookie" Jarvis by two wings in a two-minute overtime round, the first in 10 years.

SONYA THOMAS
Spills Her Guts!

An interview by Simon

- What food do you enjoy so much that you always want to eat more?

- Have you ever heard of a food-eating contest? What foods were included?

She weighs less than 100 pounds but can eat more food in one sitting than just about any other human being on the planet. Sonya Thomas, a.k.a. "The Black Widow," has broken more than a dozen world eating records. She is considered one of the world's best competitive eaters. So, what does it take to become a speed-eater?

CHECKPOINT

What different foods do you think Sonya has eaten in all the contests?

SIMON: So, what made you decide to start competing in eating contests?

SONYA: Well, I've always been a very competitive person, not just at eating, but at all sports. I just don't like losing. If I lose, I feel terrible. I was watching the World Hot Dog Eating contest on TV in 2003 and wanted to see how I would do. So, I went to the website and signed up for the contest. I ate 30.5 hot dogs in 12 minutes and finished fourth in my first year, and that's how I started.

---

a.k.a.: *also known as*

SIMON: That's a lot of dogs! How do you train for eating contests?

SONYA: I try to stay in shape and I try to stretch my stomach. I run on the treadmill for close to two hours a day. I'm a manager at Burger King and I'm always on my feet moving around. I also go to all-you-can eat buffets whenever I can. I usually only eat one really big meal a day, as well. If I'm at work, I'll eat a Chicken Whopper, with large fries, large chicken nuggets, and a diet soda. And that's all I'll eat for the day.

SIMON: Hmmm ... I wish my parents would let me eat like that. You're a pretty small person — you weigh less than me. How do you manage to eat all that food?

SONYA: Well, the size of the person doesn't really matter in competitive eating. What's important is the size of the person's stomach. I am in good shape and have a large stomach. Because I don't have a lot of fat around my tummy, my stomach has lots of room to stretch during an eating competition.

SIMON: You've set world records for eating chicken wings, cheesecake, oysters, and a bunch of other stuff. What was the hardest record to set?

SONYA: Probably the cheesecake eating. I ate 11 lb. of cheesecake in nine minutes. It was hard to eat because the crust was super dry. When I finished, my throat was super sore and my stomach totally hurt. I almost had to go to the emergency room. I ended up throwing it all up. That's the only time I've thrown up from eating. The record I'm most proud of is the oysters. I ate 432 of them in 10 minutes and I think I could've eaten even more.

SIMON: Yikes! That's totally cool! What kind of tips would you give for a kid interested in getting into competitive eating?

SONYA: I don't think I would recommend it. Competitive eating can be very dangerous in many ways. If you try eating chicken wings, it's easy to choke on the bones. For kids, it's not such a good idea, because their bodies aren't properly developed yet. I'd wait until you reach the age of 18 to 21. But if you just want to have some fun, start out eating something softer like pie or cake that isn't so easy to choke on. And just do it once in a while. Don't try eating as much as you can every day.

SIMON: What's the best thing about being one of the world's top eaters?

SONYA: Well, mostly just the recognition I get. I don't get much money for setting eating records. But it's neat that lots of people recognize me now when they see me. Probably 60 percent of the people out there think competitive eating and eating contests are really stupid. But eventually, I'd like to be thought of as an international sports star, like Tiger Woods or Michael Jordan.

WOW!

The International Federation of Competitive Eating (IFOCE) manages eating contests throughout the world. The IFOCE helps keep the sport safe and fun.

Here are some IFOCE record holders. You may be shocked at how much and what they chose to eat!

EWW!

DONALD LERMAN
Baked Beans
6 pounds baked beans
1 minute, 48 seconds

SONYA THOMAS
Cheesecake
11 pounds cheesecake
9 minutes

OH MY!

YUCK!

DONALD LERMAN
Butter
7 quarter-pound sticks
salted butter
5 minutes

ALLEN GOLDSTEIN
Bologna
2.41 pounds bologna
6 minutes

YIKES!

ERIC BOOKER
Burritos
15 BurritoVille burritos
8 minutes

GROSS!

DOMINIC CARDO
Beef Tongue
3 pounds 3 ounces
pickled beef tongue whole
12 minutes

SONYA THOMAS
Asparagus
5.75 pounds Tempura
deep fried asparagus spears
10 minutes

WOW!

wrap up

1. On a chart, list the characteristics about Sonya. Sonya likes to _____; Sonya tries _____; Sonya wants to _____; Sonya wishes she _____.

2. Which foods on the WOW! list would you not want to try? Why?

3. The measurements on the list are in standard. Convert them to metric. Check your answers with a partner.

WEB CONNECTIONS

Visit the IFOCE at **www.ifoce.com** and read some of the other records that have been created. Choose three and share them with your group.

In a small group, discuss: Why do schools forbid chewing gum? Why do kids seem to enjoy chewing gum? What do you do with your chewing gum when it has lost its flavor? What do your parents think about chewing gum?

BURSTING THE BUBBLE ON CHEWING GUM

Do you ever wonder what it is about chewing gum that gives you hours of chewing enjoyment? Why is it that the flavor disappears long before you get bored from blowing bubbles and chewing? Keep reading to find out what gum is made out of and why we can chew it for so long.

A Bit of History

Before World War II, chewing gum was made from chicle and flavors. Chicle is sap that comes from a tree. It is a form of rubber. Think of rubber bands. When you chew on rubber bands (*gross!*) they don't dissolve — and neither does chicle. Chicle is a bit softer and hardens and softens according to temperature.

Chicle practically became non-existent after the war, so scientists were forced to come up with a new resin (tree sap or rubber). Since then, gum bases have been made from various natural and unnatural resins. All of them become softer when heated and harder when cold, just like chicle.

Chew on This

Enough of the history lesson. The main ingredients in chewing gum are gum base, sugar, corn syrup, softeners, flavoring, and coloring. Gum base is mostly plastic and rubber, but it also might have latex which is a natural ingredient. Natural latex, such as chicle, is the sap from trees in the rainforest. Gum manufacturers like to keep their exact recipes secret.

So what you should have learned is that the reason gum doesn't dissolve in your mouth is because you are chewing on a wad of rubber and/or latex with a bit of flavoring. This also means that when you swallow gum, it won't be digested so it comes out in one piece. It will, however, stay inside you for a few days.

CHECKPOINT

Do you swallow the gum you chew? Should you?

Bubble Gum Alley

Ever wondered what to do with chewed bubble gum after the taste is gone? The town of San Luis Obispo in California has a unique solution — stick it in the Bubble Gum Alley! The brick walls are coated with thousands of chewed bubble gums! Locals suspect the tradition started over 40 years ago when some school kids stuck their globs on the walls.

wrap up

1. Invent a way of dealing with all the gum that has been chewed in your school. Present your invention to your class.

2. How could chewing gum be good for your teeth? Write your answer as an ad for chewing gum.

Pancake Fever

warm up

What are the differences among pancakes, waffles, flapjacks, crepes, and burritos?

Pile on the pancakes
Hot from the pan.
Pour on the syrup
As fast as you can.

Pat on the butter
Grab fork and knife.
Attack those babies
For the meal of your life.

More of the pancakes,
Heaped on my plate,
First there were four,
Then there were eight.

Should I try twelve
In this pancake race?
Four more please,
I found some space.

Wowee! Wowee!
Oh the pain,
The plate is clean,
(Am I insane?)
Hold the pancakes,
I may cry,
There's no more room

in

this

pancake

guy.

wrap up

1. Read the poem aloud as a group. When will you speed up? When will you slow down? How will you end the poem?

2. How many pancakes are in the picture? How many could you eat?

3. Imagine you had a pancake stand. Create a poster to make people want to buy your pancakes.

ACKNOWLEDGMENTS

The publisher gratefully acknowledges the following for permission to reprint copyrighted material in this book.

Every reasonable effort has been made to trace the owners of copyrighted material and to make due acknowledgment. Any errors or omissions drawn to our attention will be gladly rectified in future editions.

Tom Glazer: "On Top of Spaghetti." Permission courtesy of Songs Music Inc.

"Bursting the Bubble on Chewing Gum" from www.kidzworld.com. Permission courtesy of Kidzworld Media.

"Sonya Thomas Spills Her Guts!" from www.kidzworld.com. Permission courtesy of Kidzworld Media.

QUIZ

MIND YOUR MANNERS!

How would you rate your table manners? Take this quiz to find out.

ANSWERS

1. b)
2. c)
3. a)
4. b)
5. a)
6. c)
7. a)
8. b)
9. c)